Prose Kills

Prose Kills

A Wake-up Call from the Fringe

JOHN BRIGGS

RESOURCE *Publications* • Eugene, Oregon

PROSE KILLS
A Wake-up Call from the Fringe

Resource Publications
An Imprint of Wipf and Stock Publishers
199 W. 8th Ave., Suite 3
Eugene, OR 97401

www.wipfandstock.com

PAPERBACK ISBN: 978-1-7252-6162-4
HARDCOVER ISBN: 978-1-7252-6161-7
EBOOK ISBN: 978-1-7252-6163-1

Manufactured in the U.S.A.   03/02/20

Contents

Introduction

I HAVE NOTHING AGAINST prose except that it is not poetry, and that is reason enough to distrust it.

It is a little disingenuous to write the introduction to a book of poetry in prose, especially a book titled *Prose Kills*. But sometimes the problem really is a nail, and a hammer is the only tool that will solve it. So, let's start pounding.

I should title this section "Reintroduction," not because you have read all of this before, but because I have written this introduction at least three times. That's how hard it is for a poet to write prose. The words always want to jump to poetry and take flight. It's like an entomologist trying to pin a living butterfly to a specimen card. Can't be done. And it shouldn't be, even if it could. You must kill the butterfly first. Anything else is unethical and impractical. Unethical because the butterfly is suffering and impractical because it isn't "holding still." And there you have it. To maintain an ethical position and observe a thing in stasis, prose, like science, must kill the thing it studies.

But enough about my problems as a poet. I will do my best to lay out in prose what I think a poet does and try not to maim or kill anything in the process.

Let's start by defining what prose and poetry are and how they are different. The typical dictionary definitions are as misleading as they are incomplete because they define the two based on their appearance on the page or their sound when spoken. For example, prose is written or spoken language in its ordinary form, without metrical structure, and poetry is written or spoken language that uses meter, rhyme, line break, and wordplay. In other words, poetry is poetry because it looks and sounds like poetry and prose is prose because it looks and sounds like prose. But these definitions are circular and assume we already know what prose and poetry are. These definitions are also prefect examples of prose pretending it knows a thing or two about poetry when it clearly doesn't.

Poetry comes from the Ancient Greek 'poieo' meaning, I create. It is the language of creation, of bringing something into this world that did not previously exist here. It is the language Jesus used to feed five thousand people with five loaves of bread and two fish.

Prose comes from the Latin, 'prosus' meaning, straightforward or direct. Prose is the language of science and commerce, the language people use to manipulate, examine, explain, evaluate, and distribute that which already exists in this world. It is the language Grubhub would use to deliver fish and chips from Skippers to five thousand people.

Poetry brings new things into being and exercises authority over existing things by honoring the mystery that connects language and being. Prose denies this mystical connection and, instead, exerts control over things by force. Prose is limited to the surface of things, without any way of getting to the mystery inside them. In short, poetry brings the things to life that prose dissects, killing them in the process.

So, what exactly is a poem, and why would a poet want to write it? One word: access. Let me give you an example from my own experience. As an undergraduate, I wrote a paper for an English class explaining why I no longer considered myself a poet. To do so, I sat down at a table in the college library and created a mental image of the world and the poet's place in it. What I came up with was this:

> The world is a collection of atoms in colloidal suspension sloshing about inside a washing machine. The washing machine is traveling through time and space and spinning on its axis. Finally, the washing machine tumbles as it does so. The poet sits at the center of the washing machine and navigates the different motions until he stands outside of time and space, where nothing moves, and he can take the hand of the eternal. This connection is brief. As the machine continues to move, the coordination of the motions breaks down, and the poet is pulled back inside it.

The above paragraph looks and smells like prose. There are no poetical conceits of language—no rhythm, no rhyme, no line breaks, no elevated language—just the straight-forward, no nonsense progression of thought from point A to point B. But something unexpected happened when I finished writing the paragraph and looked up from the page. The entire room—the stacks of books, the tables, the carrels with the students in them, bending over their assignments—spun slowly around me. Startled, I blinked and shook my head until the swirling stopped. As I sat there, I asked myself, "Can I do that again?" To find out, I put my head down and concentrated again on my image of the poet sitting at the center of a swirling world. When I looked up, the room was spinning again. That's when I realized that I had cracked open a door and was standing on the threshold between our skinny world of chaos and decay and the fat world of the eternal. I would like to tell you that I entered the fat world and had a good talk with the immortals, but I didn't. Instead, I finished the paper on why I was no longer a poet and turned it in. It came back from the professor with the remark written in red, "You are doing what poets do."

I relate this story for three reasons. The first is to demonstrate that not all paragraphs are prose and not all verse is poetry. The business that the piece of writing is carrying out determines whether it is poetry. And the business of poetry is to grant access to a world outside our own that is otherwise inaccessible (This flies in the face of a great many contemporary poems that are themselves inaccessible. It's as if the reader needs a "pre-poem" to crack open the door into these.).

My second point is that poetry and prose are violent acts, but the kingdoms they assail are different. Poetry assaults the fat world—the kingdom of heaven, while prose attacks the skinny one—the kingdom of earth. The results of these assaults are as different as the kingdoms they assault. Poetry cracks open a door to another world, prose manipulates things in the existing one. Poetry (the act of creating something new) builds a bridge that allows commerce between the fat world and the skinny one. Prose limits itself to the allocation and movement of resources in the skinny one. Poetry is an expansive and open-ended work of the spirit and soul. Prose is a reductive and restrictive work of the ego that only sees a world of lack. Poetry creates twelve baskets of leftovers from five loaves of bread and two fish. Prose ignores the mystery and fights over the leftovers.

Finally, the fat world wants to be discovered. If it does not invite assault, neither does it actively defend against it. The skinny world, on the other hand, is impenetrable and repels every assault against it. The fat world reveals its depth, the skinny one hides its thinness. Let me use an analogy to illustrate the difference. Poetry writes an acorn, breaks the surface of the ground, and inserts the acorn into the soil where it is dark and moist. Then it waits for the mystery to take place. Underground, the seed begins to germinate, to die as an acorn and become an oak. Prose, on the other hand, tries to get at the mystery by cutting through the surface of the acorn until it becomes a pile of tiny pieces, each with a surface of its own, and the mystery is nowhere to be found. In other words, poetry reveals the mystery by letting the acorn die. Prose loses the mystery by killing the acorn.

Let me warn any potential writers who are reading this—poetry is dangerous. After my experience in the University library, I walked away from the threshold without crossing over and went back to my ordinary life. Or I tried to. As it turns out, you can go back to your old life, but you can never return to it. The poetic part of you still stands at the threshold asking, "Should I go in?" The rational, prose part of you (your ego) answers, "If you go in, you will die there."

After wrestling with this issue for forty seven years I can finally tell you, that if you are a poet, you must enter. It is your destiny. And, that your ego is also right, you will never come back out. But it's better to die a whole being in a terrifying world, than to die a fractured being in a safe one.

The American heart is full of prose. It is the language America speaks to itself and others. "Let's dam the rivers and build concrete ditches to move water quickly and efficiently to the fields and faucets of America. We'll automate the production of food and crisscross the country with turnpikes and freeways to distribute it. We'll build bigger homes and acres of storage units to stockpile our stuff against the day of evil. Finally, we'll build fences to protect ourselves from "the tired, the poor, the huddled masses yearning to breathe free, the wretched refuse from the world's teeming shores, the homeless and the tempest tossed."

And don't think the church is any different. I say a few unflattering things about the church in the pages of this book, and I don't want you to think they are accidental. The church is as full of prose now as at any time in its history. The Ten Commandments have replaced the beatitudes and parables of Jesus, law and order is valued over love and mercy. At times, the church acts more like the Mistress of the Skinny World than the Bride of Christ. The last thing the church needs is flattery.

To be a poet in America or in the church is to be a caddisfly larva in a concrete ditch. You don't have enough debris to build a protective case, and the water is full of hungry fish. In short, you are the prey.

The following poetry chronicles my journey over the threshold between the skinny and the fat worlds. Some of the poems, like "Where Seas Go to Dry" kept me awake at night because of the future they reveal. It took me over a week to commit to paper one of the lines in "Rites of Passage," not because I couldn't come up with the words, but because I knew that writing them down meant I would be crossing a line I could not uncross and entering a world from which I could not return. These poems came at a cost. But I would not unwrite them even if I could. Others juxtapose the fat world with the skinny one, while still others don't do anything but move the soul in a way the intellect cannot comprehend.

Some of these poems trail off without resolving. But that's ok, not all weapons come to a point.

CLOUDS ARE NOT FOR EATING

"Clouds are not for eating," Neva said.
"Not in the Skinny world," I replied.
"But in the Fat world, they are delicious.
And the rainbows taste like gum drops."

So, we spent the afternoon
Nibbling on cotton candy clouds
Dipped in a blueberry sky.
And in the evening, we nestled down
On the back of a coal black swan,
Gliding across a lake of stars,
And dreamt the dreams of the innocents.

. . . .

Never forget, little Neva,
That your house may be in the Skinny world,
But your home is in the Fat one.

THE FIELDS OF MY FATHERS: A LULLABY

I

Weary of working
The fields of my fathers,
I look from the furrows
To the evening sky,
Where a tourmaline meadow,
Full of flowers of light,
Bends beyond the dull rim of the world.

Don't worry my children,
I will go there tonight
And build me a barn of wood and stone
To harvest the little lights into.
There they will glow
As a snow-white rose
With a blossom of flame
And petals of fire.

II

Weep, my children, wail for the world.
Without the stars,
The moon won't know which way to wander
Over the empty amethyst meadow,
And the sun will have no one to follow.

The sky will grow black as anthracite,
The earth even blacker.
And in those barren fields of your fathers,
The undying worm who feeds in the dark
Will feast on the souls of the dead forever.

THE CRY OF THE CURLEW

I

The cry of the curlew
Harries my heart,
Carries me,
Clutching twilight to my breast,
Over the evening estuary.

Over the houses on the shore,
Leaking light into empty streets.
Over the thud of booted feet,
Stomping mud off on the floor.
Over the slamming of a door.

Over a bed with fevered sheets
And a little one lying there,
Past a tiny, lifeless hand
Cradling a tattered teddy bear.

Over the Chapel at Calendas Heath
Where vesper bells toll me home
To a gray stone rising from the loam
And a coffin underneath.

The singing swells inside the nave,
And children, snuggled in their beds,
Breathe a sigh of relief,
For Weeping Mary has finished her rounds
And is safely back in her grave.

II

O little one, don't fear the grave,
Or the bell that tolls you to it,
For a coffin is a leaky thing,
And one day a curlew robed in light
Will call you out with a cry,
And carry you, clutching your teddy bear,
Over the evening estuary
To a land behind the sky.

LILIES

The long, green lilies of Cohrums Veil
Wave in the wind, bend in the breeze,
Over the graves of the innocents:
The little ones who died without sins,
Torn apart in the womb
Before taking a breath.

But as stately as these lilies are,
As gallant in green with crowns of white,
They will pale when compared
To the robes of the innocents
When they rise up to judge over the world,
Over the living and the dead.

WHERE SEAS GO TO DRY

I

A trout rises toward the moon
And sinks back
Without breaking the surface of the lake
Or rippling a ring.
A slithering thing—
Perhaps a black and yellow garter snake,
Or maybe a diamondback—
Uncoils in the room.

How sharp the sting

II

I've seen the sun peeled like an orange,
And watched the moon lower its ladders—
Pale, luminous—
Like strands of DNA against the black waste of space.

That isn't Jacob's head resting on the stone,
And those aren't angels gibbering from the rungs.

III

Wizards peep and mutter
Over a stingy earth that will not yield her dead.

The willow above my head
Weeps at the slightest provocation,
And hyenas in the wadi laugh
At the sound of soil cracking.
But I know things over which the willow will not weep
And jokes that make hyenas cry.

Stars twinkle in the evening sky
Above a black mare and a roan
Approaching from the east.

Along the jetty, wet with spray from a gray-green sea,
An old hag cackles at
The billowing of the sails.

In Wales
A wind moans through the chimney pots,
As a tavern owner dips his thumb
Three times in a mug of ale
And turns the lanterns up.
"On nights like these in Bwlchgwyn
It's difficult to read the signs."

IV

Merchants stand aside and cry,
"This is not the way these seas were meant to dry."

V

In the square a fisherman
Flakes the scales from his fingers into the fire
And wraps his cloak a little tighter.

"I'd leave the seas forever
For a glimpse o' me bonny Heather
Kickin' her heels up o'er the lea,
If it weren't for the song of the mermaid
Playing 'Oceans of Love' in me forehead
When e'er I go down to the sea."

"You are one of them," the maiden, America, cries,
"Your breath smells like a gooey duct
And gives you away."

"Darn your socks, I don't know what you mean,
I am the egg man."

"We are the leg men,
And your eyes leave amber footprints."

"Dam your streams,
It's not what it seems,
I am the walrus."

"Goo goo g'joob."

Near Cock's Crow Inn
A hole opens up
And sucks the fisherman in.

VI

In Bellevue's padded rooms,
Inmates sley the reed
And thread the heddle,
Weaving angels into windows,
Knitting hinges.

Just north of east and down the hall,
Two doctors and a nurse
Scrabble at a door
For sips of fabricated light
And a skein of petits fours.

They all have guessed the unthinkable:
There is no floor.

I would not worry if the vision were a long way off,
For another time on a distant street.
I could settle back in my easy chair and rest,
Knowing that the bodies
Twisting in the heat
Were the great grandchildren of a generation
I would never meet.
But I, too, have guessed the unthinkable,
And know it isn't so.

The time has come for the testing of the churches.

Blessed are those who make it to the joining together of the holy ones.

VII

Drawn to the aroma of roasting fish,
The fisherman crawls from the sea,
Up the beach of a desert island,
To a ring of fire in the sand.
There a man with eyes of heather,
Holy hands, and amber feet
Beckons him to eat.

"How many times do you love me?"

The fisherman answers, "Three."

"Feed my sheep."
So it is that an island encircles the ocean,
And the sand swallows the sea.

Thus endeth the burden of the desert of the sea.

VIII

An eagle rises toward the wind
And sinks back
Without breaking the surface of the air
Or rippling the light.
How bright
His smile is, there,
Where the lilies lack
The will to break the skin.

THE REALM OF THE HERON

I

How many times did Cyraxes the Mede
Cast himself into the ocean,
Only to wash up on the same beach,
Before he turned his back on the sea
And headed inland?

Some say he made the decision alone
After consulting the innards of a sea bird.
But I know that isn't so.
He was invited in by an old man in a linen robe, crying,
"Welcome to the Realm of the Heron.
Come, take this lance,
There is much to do."

I since have seen Cyraxes,
Barking from the crags like an old dog,
Or rooting through reeds by the river
After water snakes and frogs.
For I, too, have heard the cry,
And have answered the call
Of the old man with a lance,
His head wrapped in a linen cowl,
Crying, "Before you can talk,
You must learn to howl."

II

The heron's call is primal,
Prehistoric, mythical,
Like Cerberus barking in a hollow log,
Or the Minotaur bellowing
Somewhere in the labyrinth.
It's hard to believe such a sound
Could come from a bird.

But the heron is not just any bird.
It is the messenger of the gods,
And the guide for those
Who would seek to find themselves
In solitude and silence.

Perhaps, when I have followed the heron to myself,
And have returned to the world of trade and commerce,
My voice will sound just as primal and discordant,
And people will say,
"We did not know that such a sound
Could come from the throat of a poet."

A WALL IN PHYLISTIA

*"For the vision is yet for an appointed time,
but at the end it shall speak, and not lie."*

I

A wall in Phylistia.
A bell in San Vitoria.
A word whispered in absentia,
And all the windows of the world swing open,
Their curtains billowing in the breeze.

A wedding gown flows beneath the trees,
The rustle of a wedding gown across the knees.

II

That chirp in the dust,
What songs it sings!
What heart black harp of beetle wings brings
To the sentry watching wide-eyed
In the low gate,
When every sound not sung
Stops short the singing
And throttles in the throat
The watchman's breathing
With firm-fingered fear.

It is not as it was a year
Ago when hymns of peace,
Borne from chinks in the old stone wall,
Sang noble heads a-nodding.
When the wind pooled heat in shadows—
Those black and burnt-out ashes of the sun's passing—
And the stones stayed warm well into evening.
No.
It is not like that.

Then, these gilded halls
Were worthy guarding,
When a fine warrior's lidless eyes
Meant others inside lidded.
Now we crouch when red war threatens
And the crouching is in vain.

Which stone broke first?
Which beam was first to crack?

III

How shall anyone sing the Lord's song
When all the lands are strange?

IV

Let me not stagger at the vision.
Take my hand lest I stumble.
And, if I fall, forget not thy servant,
Mumbling in the dark
In an unknown tongue.

I will live and die as my vision says
And take my place among the prophets,
For as the vision goes,
So go the people.

THE BEGINNING OF SPARROWS

I

Broaches grace the feathery breast of the beast
"Delivering Quality, Variety and Value"
To the rostrums of the world.
Try to keep an open mouth.

At the end of the alley
A shadow casts a man
With hatfully hair
And a dreadful of dreams.
It's about to get real
In this Odious Theater,
Where all the world's a play
And the actors merely the stage.

The beginning of sorrows is the smell of umber burning,
Or lumber.

Take a dry stick.
Or a number.
You pick.

II

These winter seeds,
Dropped, one-by-one, from blackened weeds,
Along the snowy riverbank,
Possess the faith to die.
Do you and I,
Encrusted in our shells,
Have the trust
To crack the husks of solitude and thrust
Rust-red roots down
Through empty air?

Is it truly faith if it isn't tested unto death?

III

I will not make this easy for you—
This business of dying.
You've called down fire from a sundered sky,
Sipped blood from the martyr's cranium,
Worshipped the dragon as it thundered by,
But, you have not yet to the dark tower come.
You have not yet to darkness come.

IV

Who are these tattered rags
Stooped, stumbling, three-by-three
In endless line beneath the trees?
What vapor rustles through these clothes,
And shakes the sleeves where no wind blows?

If you would know—
They who suffer the seven woes,
These unraveled knots are those.

V

In the square the witness sings—

"Now I lay me down to sleep
For a time, times, and half a time
In the grave of the Headless Kings.
But, in the morning, I shall rise
To infinite light and angel wings—"

While the tolerant tear at him.

VI

Sparrows nesting, resting,
Nestled, bright-eyed over speckled eggs,
Five more things for God to count
When the coiling serpent flicks
Its forked tongue into the sticks.

Nudging my neighbor in the pew, I whisper,
"I am the voice of One,
Crying in the suburbs,
Weeping in the willows,
Sobbing.
I am the hand of a reluctant prophet stretched above the fire,
Shaking snakes into the flames.
How many snakes will it take
To wake you?"

"Don't you know you are worth many sparrows? . . .
But not all of them."

THE FEATHERS OF THE HOLY ONES

How dare you ruffle the feathers of the holy ones,
Nesting,
Resting their heads in their feather beds?
Who gave you entrance to their rooms,
Those sheet-rocked tombs,
Dotting the hillsides of suburbia?

Stop trying to rouse them. Let them lie,
For the journey before them is steep.
And they will need a good night's sleep,
Ere they wake to stumble and fall
And, just maybe, to stand.

DIRECTIONS

North

Something stirs in the North,
The ice is waking.
At dawn
Stone giants, frozen under ice fields for millennia,
Stretch and yawn,
And a subterranean breath whistles through
Their schisty teeth.
Something new,
And yet foreseen,
Is rising into view.

South

Who can sing the song of the South?
What throat can breath the ancient vowels?
What tongue articulate its consonants?
Ten thousand chariots creak and rattle north
To join the dance of the nations,
But none can hear it.
The words are foreign, the tune atonal,
And the drums, throbbing to the rhythm of the heart,
Mask the beat.

Everyone expects
They'll put on "a pretty good show."
No one suspects
The South has found the chord of unmaking
And, with their backs to the wall,
Will sound it.

East

Ah, the East, the mysterious East:
That pudgy woman lolling on a scaly beast.
Wail, you merchants, weep with sorrow,
She's here today and gone tomorrow.

West

In the West, a post-reptilian man—
Dreadlocked,
And armed with savage science—
Headlocks
The church and cries,
"I have grown, my friend,
And you have not.
I shed you like a snakeskin."

Defrocked,
The saints are poured out on the ground
Like water.

Nowhere

My father always said,
"Keep your directions straight
If you want to survive."
But he never said what to keep
When survival was no longer
Part of the discussion.

THE WAY, THE TRUTH, AND THE LIFE

I

I am caught on the thorns,
Torn in the tangle,
And twisting just pulls me farther in
To a place I don't want to go,
To a place at the roots of things
Where flesh turns to bread,
Blood turns to wine,
And skeletons mingle with leaf mold and dirt.

II

Tendrils and rootlets twine through my body,
Seeking out joints
Where the soil is rich,
And I am drawn slowly into the radix,
Becoming one with the taproot of hell.

III

I waken to sunlight and the fragrance of roses,
And the feel of a finger
Impaled on a thorn.
Rising to look, I see the hand of my father
Picking a bloom
From the verdant foliage,
And a drop of red blood staining the petals.

And the evening and the morning were the third day.

ON EDGE: THE RUPTURE OF THE CHURCH

The scalpel flickers over flesh.
The edge approaches,
The edge that cuts but does not heal,
The edge that divides, not into two but into many,
And turns our unity into fairy tales
The toothless elders maffle to the toothless young.
Only then, when the all becomes the many,
And the many kill the few,
Can the one who comes before the one who is to come
Recast the world in his own image. So. . .

Sit back, relax, and bite down on a bullet—
This is going to hurt like hell.

THE WAY

Away from, walk,
The cell door that's always locked,
The barred windows,
Out-looking on a puckered sky
Spitting snow.
Bid the banished lands goodbye.

Pack a lunch, Boy,
Your way through darkness lies
And requires the letting go
Of old light,
Known roads.
And the turning away from ideas
To embrace the things themselves.

But, tread lightly,
For whispered is the promise
Between what is and isn't,
And few there be who hear it.

AN EVENING IN THE CITY OF THE DEAD

The city at night is cadaverous.
Buildings, the empty skulls of commerce,
Stare into the street with black, lidless sockets.
Life has ebbed back into the suburbs
And left a body on the beach, pale, almost luminous,
And hollow as an echo.
Street cleaners,
The only things out at this hour,
Move down the streets with little mechanical stops and starts, instinctively,
Like hermit crabs scouring the beach of debris.

To walk these streets (not many do)
Is to enter the city of the dead.
But not the city of the damned—here are no ghosts,
No horned tormentors, no over-arching malevolence,
Just the dead,
Vacant as the shed
Skins of ancient reptiles.
It is a land as empty of intent
As a dead man's hand,
Brushing up against your foot in a lake.

This is a place of solitude.
A place where nothing moves of its own volition,
Where sound lacks the will to bounce.
This is the city where the Other never comes,
Where you could lose your way
And none would ever know that you were missing.

But this is also the place where silence listens to silence,
Where mirrors reflect upon themselves
Where you can find yourself—
Naked, alone, free from shackles and conventions,
Fatally human—
And sit down to a quiet meal.
'Till life flows in with the rising sun
And washes you away.

RITES OF PASSAGE

I

Bringing light out of darkness,
Wringing life from death,
I take my place on the stone seat
That lies at the center of madness.
There, I negotiate a path
Through the seven motions
To a place outside of time and space
And take the hand of God.

II

Aligning the five stations,
I move toward the darkness in the flame,
Past the monster in the darkness,
Through the door that must never be opened,
To a stool at the center of hell
Where I sip the scalding tears of Satan
From a wooden chalice.

III

Struggling with the gravity of my humanity, I stagger,
And stumble toward the redemption of God.

GAT SHEMANIM

A garden waits at the end of things
Where grow the olive, and the sycamore,
And the tree of life.
But there is another garden before it—
Small, deserted, and overgrown,
With brambles that hide a stone
Stained with blood.

The only way to enter the Garden at the End of Things
Is to spend an evening in the little garden
And then to cross the perilous wilderness
That separates them.

Everyone longs to enter the Garden at the End of Things—
The ground around it is littered with the bones of those who have tried—
But few are willing to enter Gat Shemanim, the little garden,
And fewer yet actually do.
    —from the "Book of Shards"

I

After the death of my father,
One of the last stabilizing influences in my life,
I found myself alone in my living room.
As I sat there, pondering what I should do next,
A vision appeared, and I saw myself in a desert,
Handing God a slip of paper
With my unwritten name upon it.

He handed back four stones and a sling
And said, "Hurl these stones as far as you can
To the North, to the South, to the East, and to the West."

I took the sling and hurled a stone to the North,
Where it sailed up toward the sky.
As I watched, the stone burst into feathers,
And, taking the form of an eagle,
Soared out of sight
Beyond the horizon.

Then, I hurled the second stone to the South.
It sailed up for a ways
And fell back to the earth,
Where it burst into a ball of fur,
And, taking the shape of a coyote,
Loped out of sight
Over the horizon.

I took the third stone and slung it to the East.
It rose toward the morning sun
Where it burst into feathers
And, taking the form of a raven,
Flapped its way beyond the horizon.

Taking the fourth stone, I slung it to the West
Where it skipped across the ground
Before bursting into scales
And, taking the form of a snake,
Slithered under a rock.

"I have done as you asked.
I have hurled the four stones
To the North, to the South,
To the East, and the West."

"And what did you see?"

"The first stone turned into an eagle and soared to the North.
The second stone became a coyote and loped to the South.
The third stone tuned into a raven and flapped to the East."

"And what of the fourth stone," he asked?

"It turned to a snake and slithered down a hole," I replied.

"Then that is the stone you must follow.
But we will wait for the other stones to return.
They will bring the things you need
To make your journey."

II

Early the next morning,
As I looked to the North,
A small speck rose above the horizon,
And gathered itself into a great eagle
As it approached.
It clutched a lance of blue ice in its talons
Which it dropped at my feet
Before wheeling upward and soaring back to the North.

The ice in the lance was so cold
It had formed a skin
That kept the lance from freezing whatever it touched
And from melting even in the desert heat.
Holding it, I could feel a faint pulse
As if I were holding the frozen heart of the North.

A howl brought me around,
And I turned to see a coyote,
Loping toward me from the South.
It carried a key in its mouth
Which it dropped at my feet.
Then, turning with a yip,
It loped back the way it had come.

The key was attached to a leather necklace
And though small, was heavy for its size, and carved
With the image of a snake biting its own tail.

As I marveled at the intricacies of this key,
A raucous cry to my left startled me,
And I turned to see a raven
Walking toward me with a ring

In its beak.
Three feet from me,
The raven dropped the ring.
Then, giving me a sideways glance
With a pitch-black eye,
The raven cried once more.
And, rising from the ground,
She flapped away toward the East.

The ring was black
And set with a small stone.
At first glance, the stone appeared smooth,
With a dull, brown surface.
But, as I held the ring,
The stone became warm,
Almost hot, to the touch,
And the surface wavered and grew clear.
Beneath it, colors danced and flickered
Like embers in a fire.

"These are the things you will need
To follow the snake.
It will become obvious as you travel
When to employ them.
Take courage. Do not fear.
I have been this way before you,
And have left the gate open."

III

On the morning of the third day,
I rose to a brilliant sun rising in the East
And a blue, cloudless sky overhead.
Turning westward, I saw my shadow
Stretched across the desert floor,
Its head resting on the stone
Under which the snake had slithered.

After placing the key around my neck
And slipping the ring on my finger,
I grabbed my lance and walked to the rock—
A chunk of brown and pink sandstone
About the size of a dining room table,
And just as flat—
Jutting over the edge of a dry wash.

I poked around under the stone with the lance,
But there was no sign of the snake.
Relieved, I started to turn
When a rock, loosened by my lance,
Tumbled from beneath the stone onto the stream bed,
Revealing a small hole.

I tore at the hole with my hands,
Pulling away rocks and dirt,
Until I stood at the entrance a cave,
Just large enough that I could crawl inside.

Not waiting, lest my courage fail,
I inched into the cave.
To my surprise and delight
It widened as I crawled
Until I was able to stand upright.
The cave was dry
And smelled of dust and pack rat nests.
The only light came from the opening behind me,
And I could see the cave extending away
Into the darkness.

I stood a moment, wondering how I was going to find my way,
When the ring on my finger began to warm,
And beams of light streaked from my fingers.
Thanks to the raven's gift,
I had light to continue my journey.

Three hundred and fifty-seven steps into the cave
I came upon a deep hole in the floor,

With a set of stairs carved into the side.
I tossed a stone into the hole
To see if I could tell how deep it was,
But no sound came back,
And the light could not pierce the darkness
Far enough to see where the bottom might be.

I don't know how many days I spent on those stairs.
There was no way to mark the passing of time.
I descended and slept, descended and slept,
Until I lost count of the number of cycles.
I forgot the smell of sage after a rain,
The warmth of a summer breeze upon my face,
The communal twitter of sparrows nesting in the evergreens.
My world became an endless stairway,
A blank stone wall that gave back no reflection,
And a growing loneliness
That gnawed at my soul like a rat.
But all the while I never grew hungry or thirsty.
More than once I thought of throwing myself
Off the stairs and into the abyss,
But something, either hope or fear, always stayed me.
Finally, when I was at the point of despair,
The light from the raven's ring
Flickered and went out.

Blackness as heavy as a thick, wool blanket covered me,
And I wept like a lost child.

I don't know how long I sobbed,
But when I stopped,
I could faintly see the wall beside me
And the steps descending.
At first, I thought my eyes had adjusted to the darkness,
But then, I noticed that the wall of the cave opposite me
Flickered as if from a fire.
And, looking down into the hole,
I saw a faint light coming up from the bottom.

A joy I hadn't felt since entering the cave
Welled up in me,
And I bounded down the stairs,
Two or three at a time,
Until I reached a small ledge around the opening
Through which light poured upward and past me
In a flickering column.

I knelt on that ledge and peered into the hole.

IV

Help me, Spirit of the Flame,
Give me fire-forged words
To tell the wondrous things I saw there
At the center of the world.

The hole into which I peered
Opened onto a spherical room
With five great oaks growing at equidistant points
Out of the rounded wall.
Their leafy branches met and mingled
At the center of the room.
(One could liken it to a child's snow globe
With trees growing inward toward the center
from various locations on the glass.)

At the center, where the branches met,
A ball of fire burned,
Sending shafts of light upward in all directions
To flicker against the walls.
Occasionally, sparks flew up as well
Where they bounced at the feet of the great oaks
Like fiery acorns.
Although the fire was hot,
It did not consume the leaves of the oak,
And something dark moved at its center.

As I watched this in wonder,
I noticed other small holes in the walls of the globe.
At odd intervals, human shapes
Would fall from these holes
Into the great fire at the center.
(Although it looked as if they were rising from the ground
At the feet of the oaks,
They were falling from all directions
Down into the fire.)

"It'sss the gate to the Afterworld,
And the people you see falling into the flames
Are the sssouls of the recently dead,"
Something hissed from the ledge across from me.

Startled, I turned to face a snake staring at me from the shadows.

"The trees you sssee growing out of the walls
And meeting at the center
Are the Five Propylaea Oaks.
Their branches hold the fiery gate
Which burns among the leaves without consuming them."

"What you do now is all the same to me.
If you are a coward, flee back up the ssstairs and wait your time to die.
Then you can enter the gate as you see these others do.
But if you are brave and would know more, follow me."

With that, the snake slithered from the ledge
And dropped into the flames.

V

The gates of the Afterworld are in the fire,
Burning at the center of the earth,
Whose sparks fly up in all directions.

As I fell into the flames,
Searing heat charred my clothes to ash,

Which fell away, leaving me naked.
And still the fires burned,
Consuming what the darkness in the cave
Had not eaten.
Everything I held dear—
Every hope, dream, desire—
Turned to smoke and blew away,
Leaving my soul a smoldering cinder.
I was at the point of despair
When the lance I had forgotten I was holding
Began to warm.
I could feel the pulse inside it quicken,
And the skin around it soften and melt away,
Until I was holding a steaming shaft of ice.
The flames around me eased a bit because of the ice,
And, as the shaft began to drip and crack,
I saw a shadow standing in the flame ahead of me.
Just as the lance turned to vapor in my hand
I plunged into the shadow and fainted.

When I woke, I was lying in a long hall
That stretched away before me as far as I could see.
The walls, ceiling, and floor were carved
With strange creatures which glowed
With a pale green light
And seemed to move when seen out of the corner of my eye.

As I sat there, a human figure emerged from the darkness behind me
And ran past me down the hall.
It wore no clothes
And stared ahead with unseeing eyes as it ran.
I yelled after it, but it kept on running
As if it had not heard.

I quickly rose and gave chase,
Although half-heartedly, since I wasn't sure it was a human.
And if it were, what sort of human it would be.
As I ran, two other forms overtook me and ran past

Without slowing or responding to my cries.
These ran for a while and disappeared around a corner
As the hall took a jog to the left.

I will never forget the horror
That met me as I turned that corner.

VI

About thirty yards away
In the middle of the hall
A giant stood, blocking my way.
It was naked, hairy, gaunt, and its head nearly scraped the ceiling.
Fortunately, its back was to me
Or I surely would have cried out.
I could tell by the way its elbows moved in and out
That it was busy with something in its hands.
Turning to retreat around the corner,
I put my hand against the wall for support.
As I did so, one of the creatures carved in the wall
Coiled beneath my palm, and I gasped in surprise.

Immediately, the giant turned,
And I stood face to face
With the Titan in one of Goya's paintings.
Its eyes, yellow and luminous, flickered
Like a lantern in a gale.
I didn't sense intelligence or malice in them,
Just a great distance, as if the eyes were looking at me
From an ancient world at the dawn of time.
And then I saw that it was holding in its hands
One of the human forms that had run past me.
The human's arms and legs flailed,
And its body shook with spasms,
But it could not cry out,
For its head was missing.
Blood bubbled from the neck
And dripped from the slobbering lips of the giant.

The giant dropped the body and lunged toward me,
And surely would have had me
If it weren't for the two unfortunate human forms
That turned the corner and ran past me as the giant leaped.
Startled by the sudden appearance of these two,
The giant instinctively grabbed for them
Instead of me.
And, before he could gather his wits,
I jumped past him and raced down the hall
As if the very hound of hell were upon me.

Apparently, two souls in the hand
Are better than one in the hall,
For the giant never gave chase, but instead,
Turned his attention to them.

It was a long time before I stopped running,
And only because my lungs were burning from exertion
And from the sulfurous air of the hall.

After catching my breath,
I continued down the hall
Until I came to a wooden door
Set into the wall on my left.
It hung on great iron hinges
And was carved with the same creatures
That adorned the wall.
A round lock sat in the center of the door,
And an inscription in an unknown script
Was carved in the stone lintel above it.

"It reads, 'The Door That Mussst Never Be Opened,'" hissed the snake,
As it slithered from under the door.

"And why must it stay closed," I asked.

"It's a sssecret. But I've been inside and haven't seen
Anything amisss."

"What will happen if I open it?"

"You'll have to go inside, ssssilly."

"I mean, will anything bad happen?"

"Bad is a matter of perssspective.
You won't die if that's what you're afraid of.
Nothing dies down here.
Everything wants to,
But nothing can.
That's what makes this a Living Hell.
Not even those lost souls you saw
Being eaten by the Titan can die.
They will regenerate to be chased down the halls
By the unseen horrors they brought with them."

"SSSo, it may not be bad to open the door,
But it won't be good.
Nothing good happens here.
At least you'll know what's in there,
And why you were sent down here.
If you don't open the door,
You will have wasted a long journey,
Don't you think?"

Walking to the door, I tried the handle to see if it would turn.
It didn't budge.
I tried harder, and it still wouldn't turn. "It's locked," I said,
"So that makes the decision easy."

"It's only locked if you don't have a key, sssilly."
And with that the snake slithered back under the door.

Then I remembered the key
Given to me by the Coyote,
And my heart sank.
Could this be the key that will open the door?
Wasn't I instructed to follow the snake,
Regardless of where it went?
In my mind's eye I saw myself,
Standing on the brink of a bottomless abyss,

Knowing I was going to leap.

I took the key from around my neck,
And inserted it into the lock.
"I'll never know if I never try," I whispered,
And gave the key a turn.

Inside the door, gears turned, bars clunked,
And chains clanked,
As the key disappeared
With a snap into the lock.

Grasping the handle with both hands,
I gave it a twist, and the great door swung in.

VII

Wisps of smoke and vapor
Curled from the opening
And rose into the upper reaches of the hall,
Where they flattened against the stone ceiling
And crawled out among the arches like tentacles.

Stepping inside the door,
I could see little except shifting vapors,
Like a thin, black fog
That hid the roof and the walls
So that I couldn't guess the size of the room.
I stood there for a while,
Letting my eyes adjust to the darkness,
When at last I saw something
That looked like a stool
About one hundred yards away.
It had a light shining on it
From a source hidden in the darkness
Above it.

I moved toward it,
Knowing that it held

The object of my quest,
Though I had no idea
What it was I was questing for.

As I drew closer,
I saw that it was, indeed, a three-legged stool
With a chalice sitting in the center of the seat.
The light shining from above
Made the stool and chalice look as if they
Were made of gold.
But when I reached them,
I could see that both the stool
And the chalice were made of wood.

"It's the ssstool at the center of hell,"
The serpent said as it uncoiled
From one of the stool's legs.
"And the wooden chalice
Holds the ssscalding tears of Satan."

"You know what you mussst do,"
The snake whispered,
As it slithered away into the darkness.
"It's your dessstiny."

I would like to say I rushed to the cup
And, taking it with both hands,
Drained it,
Like one of the Arthurian knights.
But I didn't.

I paced back and forth
Around the stool.
I stood for what seemed like an eternity,
Weighing the consequences
Of drinking or not drinking the cup.
Two things I knew.
First, if I drank from that cup
I would be crossing a line I could not uncross,

And be entering a realm
From which I could not return.
And second, if I did not drink
From that cup
I would never know what it is
To be fully man.

Finally, taking the cup from the stool, I cried,
"I don't believe
That drinking from this cup
Is my destiny,
But I do believe
That drinking from this cup
Will bring me to it."
And, with a single gulp,
I drained the chalice to the lees.

VIII

I woke to a darkness so complete
That if it hadn't been
For the burning in my throat
I wouldn't have believed
I was awake.

Somewhere in the distance,
A beast howled,
And a shriek rose from the earth
To greet it.
But, oddly, I was unafraid.
Instead I felt a strength
Flow from my core.
And, with a confidence
I had never known,
I rose to my feet
And shouted,
"Let there be light."

Instantly, the air grew bright,
And I could see that I was still in the room
Where the stool had stood.
But now, instead of a wooden stool,
A great stone seat,
Hewn without hands,
Rose from the ground.
Looking around, I saw that the door
Through which I had entered the room was gone.
There was truly no way home,
And, struck by the finality of the loss,
I began to weep.

But only for a short while.
I could sense that the life I had lost
Had been replaced with something deeper,
A 'certainty' whose foundations were
Driven into bedrock,
And that I had
A great deal of work yet to do.

With that, I turned from the wall
And walked toward the stone seat.
The ground was littered with the bones
Of those slain in war.
As I walked, a voice whispered on a wind
That seemed to come from everywhere and nowhere,
"Can these bones live again?"

"Only you know," I replied.

"Prophesy to the four winds
Over these bones."
So, I did, saying,
"Let these bones live again."

At once, the bones began to rattle and move
And join, joint to joint.
Muscle covered the bones,

And flesh covered the muscle.
But they had no life.

So, I prophesied again, saying,
"Let these bodies live and breathe,"
Immediately, a wind that smelled of rain and sunlight
Blew over them,
So that they rose up a living army.

Walking through their ranks,
I took my place on the stone seat.

"Impresssive," hissed the snake,
As it slithered from beneath the seat.
"Raising up such an army.
But it will do you no good
Against the coming madnesss."

"I didn't raise the army because I needed it."
I raised the army to see if I could.
The faith to raise an army
Is more powerful than any army it raises.
And, besides, I had help."

"You will need this faith in ssspades!" the snake whispered,
As it disappeared beneath the seat.
And with that, the wind gathered to a tempest,
Catching up the soldiers
And whirling them away,
Like leaves before an autumn storm.

And still the tempest grew to a hurricane,
Howling in from all directions;
Ripping the roof off the room,
Flattening the walls,
And tearing the earth and stones from the floor,
Until the stone seat was the only stable thing
At the center of a whirling chaos
That intensified until the universe itself
Was drawn into madness.

I closed my eyes
To better see the chaos around me
And to make sense of it.

The universe swirled and eddied,
But not quite like a maelstrom,
Which has a unified, circular motion
Around an eye.
This motion was random, like a loose collection of atoms
In colloidal suspension
Sloshing about in a washing machine.
But there were other motions at work
As if that washing machine were also moving forward
Through time and space.
And as it moved, it spun on its axis like a top
And tumbled as it did so.

When I opened my eyes,
The madness had ceased,
And I found myself clothed,
And standing in a purple meadow full of yellow flowers
That glowed like votive candles
In the evening air.
And my hand was holding the hand of God.

IX

"Well done, good and faithful servant.
You have done even more than
I have asked."

"From now on,
What you write will become what is.
You will write the hard things,
Those songs that are difficult to sing
And terrible to hear,
Songs with their feet in hell
And their heads in heaven.
People will stop their ears

And cry out against you, saying,
'Silence! We cannot bear to hear such sacrilege!'
But do not fear them.
They will stumble and fall for your sake."

"Keep the raven's ring.
Its power is gone,
But it will remind you
Of the poet you have become.
And when the songs end,
And we meet again,
I will trade the ring for a white stone
With your unwritten name written on it."

"Go now,
Time is short
And you have a wilderness to cross."

At that, I woke with a start,
And found myself,
Sitting on the sofa in my living room,
And staring at the evening sun,
Setting behind the distant hills.

X

And so, the vision of Gat Shemanim ends,
And the destiny of a man begins.

THE MADNESS OF DAYLIGHT

I

Crazy trumps insane
In the wind-eaten Big Empty.

That little breeze nibbling at the sage
Gnaws my bones, sucks the marrow,
Rattles through my cranium
Like an ancient prospector,
Drilling for uranium.

I have seen my soul loping over the horizon
On the back of an antelope:
Hands full of horn,
Legs hugging the haunches,
As tight as clothes pins
Pinching wet shirts to the line.
I've heard it rooting through the willows
By the dry stream at night.

That's the way to live—
Leaving torn bits of flesh on rusted wire
And making tracks through the alkali.
But it's best to do so at night
When the heat has uncoiled from the cactus
And lies across the trail like a diamondback.

II

An empty pocket,
Nevada is the perfect place for holes.
Prospects dot the hillsides
Where old-timers tried to resurrect their dreams.
For most of them,
Lazarus had been rotting far too long
And refused to rise.

Even so,
There are places
Where old-timers never go,
Places where the snakes are velvet ropes,
And empty hopes
Are watered with free gin.

They are not fooled by the glitter of it,
They are not taken in.

So, if you pick up one of these locals,
Hitchhiking between Insanity
And "a little further in,"
Don't be offended when he chuckles at
Your praises of "Zoomanity,"
Turns a crazy eye on you, and grins:
"Just because you've been to Vegas
Doesn't mean you've seen Nevada."

WHAT IT MEANS TO CALL MYSELF A POET

To call myself a poet is
To drive a tent peg in a hurricane,
Lengthen the cords,
Strengthen the stakes,
And spread out to the left and right.

To call myself a poet is
To face a crowd of thousands
With two fish and a hoagie roll
And to gather up the leftovers.

To call myself a poet is
To affirm, "I know my place
In the scheme of things,
But you can't quite place me
Anywhere."

To call myself a poet is
To look into the mirror
And cry out with a foreign accent,
"Hey, I know djoo!
We smoked pot togyether!"
Without turning us in.

THE SPARROW AT MY FEEDER

The sparrow at my feeder
Acts as if it doesn't care that winter's coming,
As if it doesn't know that the cat,
Who isn't there today,
Could be there tomorrow.

The sparrow in my evergreen
Bobs, flicks, and twitters,
As if it makes no difference
Who won the last election,
As if the nation splintering into shards
Is of no concern at all.

The sparrow at my window
Doesn't care whether I fill the feeder.
God will provide as He has done for generations,
And it will find its meal of seeds elsewhere.

The sparrow on my headstone
Wonders how a man who had so little faith
Could be worth even one of its kind,
Let alone many.

THE LITTLE CHAPEL OF CAUSE AND EFFECT

Another morning service
At the Chapel of Cause and Effect,
And the line of people entering
Extends around the block.
Everyone is eager to hear
The sermon they've come to expect:
"If you can find the Cause,
You can control the Effect."

"If you are faithful to this tenet
And pay your tithes on time,
We will invite you down to the basement,
Where you will surely find
That every wheel in the universe
Is turned by a single crank,
And God, Himself, is chained there,
Cranking it."

Whatever.

My friends down the street at Heidegger's Pub
Take a different view:

"The world may, indeed, turn by a crank,
But, the pietistic drive it home
With a screw."

WHAT DOESN'T KILL YOU

In the desert, what doesn't rattle hisses—
Scales scrabble across the stones,
Wind whispers in the tamarisk,
Sand ripples itself into dunes.

Who can say how deep the cracks
Penetrate the skin of that dry lakebed?
Do they reach the quick?
In this heat, it is easy to believe
That these cracks could split the earth into a billion shivers
And hurl them into space to circle distant worlds.

In the desert, blood caramelizes in the brain,
And you sometimes see your soul, miles away,
Wading through mirages in search of water.
When you blink, your soul is swallowed by the fiction that lies between you,
Only to surface further off and a little to the left.
Sometimes, when you rise to go,
It whispers, "Freedom is just a bigger box to die in,"
And its gravity drags you down.

In the desert, what doesn't kill you prolongs the agony:

There aren't enough tears in the sea
To water the withered root of the world.

THE SKIES CAN'T CRY ENOUGH

The skies can't cry enough
To heal what has been done to the seas
By science.

For thousands of years
Men sailed the bright seas, brimming
With angry monsters and gods.
That was a place where a man
Could lose his life and find it.

Science has delivered us from monsters and gods
To set us adrift on a silent sea,
Choked with plastic and styrofoam.
Whatever dies there can never be found.

What hero, then, will deliver us from science?
It certainly won't be science!
We can't be that moronic!
Can we?

. . . .

"Oh, give me a wooden boat and an oar
To sail the wild and savage seas o'er,
To measure my might against the best
The heavens and depths have to offer."

ANOTHER SUNRISE IN NEVADA

In the East,
The beating of bright angel wings
Fans crimson layers of light, shimmering,
Across the domed expanse of sapphire sky.

A meadowlark on a splintered post
Warbles its reply.

Deep in the field,
A tattered hat looks up and sighs,
"Looks like rain.
And there it is in a nutshell—
What's bad for the hay,
Is good for the grain."

And the meadowlark on the splintered post
Warbles the refrain.

THIN

The world is thin as rice paper,
Thin as the skin
On the back of my hand.

(And all we know,
All we think,
All we think we know,
Is no deeper than an ink
Stain.)

Tear at the world with both hands.

The kingdom of heaven suffers violence,
And the violent take it by force.

UNITY

While we slept,
The crack became a fissure
And split the world in two.
And, on this split,
Our unity is built.

COUNSEL OF THE ROSE

It's easy to love the feathered petals, the hues,
And the drowsy fragrance on the breezes borne,
But you haven't known the counsel of the rose
Until you have pricked your finger on a thorn.

A SNARL OF SKIES

A snarl unwinds the sky
And marks the passing of another drone
On its way to asserting our indifference.
Lord, please attend to these thy mendicants.
Meet us in the Gas House.
We'll toast big food abstentions
And bless the dinner mints,
While outside the rippled earth
Crashes like the sea against
The cliffs.

FIRST ROUND PICK

I asked a wealthy matron once,
"Who is your favorite football team?"
She tilted her head back and huffed,
"I see no redeeming social value in football."
Smiling, I asked,
"Really? What could be more redeeming
Than watching a bunch of spoiled millionaires
Having at each other in an arena?"
"Oh," she laughed. "I've never looked at it that way."
"I know you haven't," I said.
"And that is why the world needs poets."

"Now, go suit up."

WAXING LISA

Waxing, Lisa cries,
"Morning lies
Are best served with a rasher of beer
And a short stack of bacon."

Waxing philosophical, Lisa sighs,
"Daylight is only moonlight
'Putting a happy face on'
In the mirror,"

Too pink to think,
Wayne waxes hypothetical,
"What if
Blah. Blah. Blah . . . ?"

Some fables are past scruting
And are only good for strewing
Across the path where ravens meet,
Or for dropping beneath the table
For the whelps to eat.
And not all of these tales told
Are old.

I urge you sons of salmon
Daughters of sleep
Attend your schools,
Count the sheep,
And trim that which dangles without provocation
From the edges.
Let it die outside the camp. . .
Like Jesus.

TO THE MAN WHO WON'T BE TAKEN

To the man who won't be taken,
Nothing can be given.
Even in the rain he finds a hidden motive,
And in the sunshine, sinister intent.

The heart of the man who won't be taken
Is a delicate rose
Clutched in an iron grip.
His soul feeds in the dark on dust,
And fear feeds on him.

To the man who won't be taken,
Love is an interrogation.
Doubt is his defense,
Rust his closing argument,
And suicide his escape
From death.

So, when the man who won't be taken
Takes your hand,
Be kind.
Everything he loves
Is slipping through his fingers
Like tiny grains of sand.

SILVER SCREEN

I am the silver screen
Onto which you project your demons.
There they dance, gibber, spit, and mock you.
When you tear at them with knives and nails,
They vanish into the gashes in the screen.

In the morning,
When you see the scars and flaps of skin
Hanging from my ribs,
You ask, "What evil spirit did this thing?"
And they jabber, "You did."

LIKE AN ACORN

Unless you die
Before you die
You waste your days
Trying to be an oak
Without ever sprouting.

Life is the struggle to be born,
And dying before Death
Is the doorway to it.

THERE ARE NO WORDLESS PLACES

There are no wordless places,
No silent pockets language hasn't probed,
Groping, maybe, for a quarter or a key,
No crevice, miles below the crust,
That God's voice, cracking,
Didn't crack
Into His articulation of basalt.
There's nowhere we can go
God's language hasn't been.

But we no longer speak it,
This language that could build a tower to the heavens,
Or, failing that, cast God's throne down to earth.

So, we wander nameless,
Barbarians, gibbering in a thousand tongues,
And tearing at creation with the jaws of science,
In hopes of opening some fantastic void
God has never whispered into,
Where we can scream,
"I am!"
To no one.
And, almost, believe it.

DRYADS

"I have cut the green woods down," little Timmy said,
"And found no dryads in them."

And I wept to hear it.

"The world has burned and turned to ash," the leafy dryads said.
"The mountains all have tumbled down.
We have searched for little Timmy,
But he could not be found."

And we wept for joy to hear it.

WHERE DID JESUS GET THE FISH?

If the universe is an isolated system,
Where did Jesus get the fish?

DRAGONS

Slaying dragons used to be so easy
Even a saint could do it.

In Spring, when the snows melt,
And the March wind blows,
The dragon in me
And the dragon in you
Rise on the wind
To make sport in the air—
While we make war on the earth.
For them it is just a game.
For us it is deadly earnest.

We can't slay each other's dragons,
We can only slay our own,
And neither of us trusts the other
To follow through.
After all, no man wants to stare
Another man's dragon in the eye,
Without having a dragon of his own.

So here we stand, facing off,
Armed to the teeth,
Year after year, age after age, war after war,
As an ashy sun sets and rises above
A blasted earth,
Groaning for the revelation of
The sons of God.

"So, what'll it be, Punk,
Are you feeling lucky?"

THE BRAIN DEATH OF THE UNIVERSE

A wake will be held in the chapel
For the brain death of the Universe
When everything reverts to mindless matter.
This will be followed by Mass
And the resurrection of the dead.
Service starts promptly
And ends a little later.

Please bring a non-perishable food item for the Barnabus fund.

THE BARK IS ON THE HOWL

Fever frets the trees,
And the bark is on the howl.
Chatter clatters in the leaves,
And roots begin to prowl.
Better stay indoors tonight,
With your eyes upon the hour,
For something evil's out there,
Seeking whom it may devour.
It's not the Wrath of God,
Which over time abates,
Nor is it Satan's ire.
It is your wicked heart that hunts you,
That, when it finds you, binds you, twig and limb,
And thrusts a torch into the pyre.

THE ANSWER, MY FRIEND

Frogs, chirping from the mud,
Breed in the reeds,
Fuck in the muck,
And brag about the size of their families,
While making the best of a bad thing.

A heron hears the boast
And picks them off,
One by one,
Until it can eat no more.

Millions of pollywogs
Wriggle, and writhe, and morph in the mire
Until the bog is a-boil with little frogs,
Eager to take their parents' places,
To chirp their own boasts to the wind.

And we are caught in the middle,
Desperately trying to maintain
This "Natural Balance" of violence
Between the number of predators and the number of prey.
To find an acceptable ratio of beetles to bark, of fangs to flesh,
Of Nazis to Jews, cowboys to Indians,
Of klansmen to niggers, Bloods to Crips,
Liberals to conservatives, lions to Christians,
Theists to atheists, bullets to children,
And caucasians to everyone else.

Because the future of the world
Is hanging in the balance,
Is twisting in the wind.

A SPECIAL KIND OF FOOL

Any fool can point, but
Can anyone how deep down say is,
Or how high's up?

Any fool can fly
When gravity'sgripsl i p s
And the universe goes hurtling
To the ends of everywhere. But,

It's a special kind of fool
Who bets his soul on matter
Which, with a little heat, dissolves
And leaves no hole to hide in.

ABSOLUTES

Tell me, Mr. Plato,
How love and hate can cast
The same shadow of a cross upon the wall
If there is no incarnation.

BRACE FOR IMPACT

History is only circular
When you view it from the bullseye.
Viewed from the side,
It is an arrow
Cracking toward the mark.

DISARMING VENUS

I

Now that we've buggered Beatrice
Who will usher us into Paradise?

What image?

All is smeared, profane, trodden under
Like pearls in a pig sty.
That which shines
Is lacquer over chipboard,
Chrome over pot metal.
Nothing is stainless.

II

Who is this whimpering thing
Casting its shadow on the body of my lover
Between the ache and the act?
Is it some forlorn child
Who will not be consoled?

I have chased it down corridors,
Past the rooms of couples,
Twining under twisted sheets,
Only to lose it
In the mirror above the mantle
In the great hall.

But still its wailing echoes through the palace
And up the chimney pipes.

III

"Hush little baby, don't say a word,
Papa's gonna buy you a mockingbird. . . ."

Sometimes a promise is the only bed to lie in,
And the hope of redemption our only comforter.

GRACES

Sometimes, when you don't think I am looking,
I watch the sunlight frame your face
As you lay your knitting on your lap
And stare into the space
That separates us.
It breaks my heart,
As you take your knitting up again,
To see such innocence and beauty torn,
A beauty that would stun the graces.
And still you soldier on
Waiting for an old knot of a man
To disentangle and come to his senses . . . .

Please forgive me,
I have been a fool.

I KNOW NOW WHAT THE SIRENS SING

Come to us, come ashore.
Let us loose the Gordian knot
That binds your soul to bone.
For we are lovely, are we not?
We will tug at the thread that dangles
Until your soul unravels
And your body becomes one with the sea.

Cast away your heavy oar,
Stained with sea and sweat.
Give up your struggle.
Surrender to the urge
To cast yourself into the tides
And tumble lifeless in the surge.
For we are ravishing brides,
And nubile, are we not?

And, if against all odds,
You crawl up on the beach,
We will peck at your eyes
And strew your bones across the sand
For you do not deserve us.
You do not deserve to be the husband
Of anyone.

But, surely, you must try
To prove worthy.
Yes, you must, before you sleep.
It is madness sailing into that black night
Not fathoming the infinite depth
Of your endless deep.

www.ingramcontent.com/pod-product-compliance
Lightning Source LLC
La Vergne TN
LVHW051705080426
835511LV00017B/2734